A l... ...isure &

JERSEY YARN
CREATIONS

20 projects to knit & crochet

Search Press

Thank you to DMC for providing us with the balls of jersey yarn and accessories.

And, thank you to L'Atelier for providing us with the beads (27 rue des plantes, 75014 Paris).

www.facebook.com/alexandresamuse
instagram.com/alexandresamuse

First published in Great Britain in 2015 by Search Press
Wellwood, North Farm Road, Tunbridge Wells, Kent, TN2 3DR

Graphic design: Anne Bénoliel-Defréville
Layout: Coline de Graaff
Photographs: Claire Curt
Styling: Sonia Roy

© Libella, Paris, 2014

This translation of *HOOOKED ZPAGETTI – Crochet et Tricot,* first published in France by LIBELLA under the imprint LTA in 2014, is published by arrangement with Silke Bruenink Agency, Munich, Germany.

ISBN: 978-1-78221-216-4

Suppliers
If you have difficulty in obtaining any of the materials and equipment mentioned in this book, then please visit the Search Press website for details of suppliers: www.searchpress.com

Introduction

I first fell in love with jersey yarn at a craft fair. I was drawn to it at first sight and immediately wanted to find out more – it wasn't long before I had made my first project, a little basket, and I was amazed at how quick and easy it was to make up!

Jersey yarn (also known as T-shirt yarn or fabric yarn) is a high-quality material, responsibly recycled from industry fabric offcuts. It is incredibly versatile and inspires me with all sorts of plans and ideas. It is great fun and easy to work.

I wanted to share my fascination with jersey yarn and so this book offers a wide range of creations for all skill levels. Whether you have never picked up a crochet hook or knitting needle before, or whether you are already an expert, there is a project here for you.

Jersey yarn creations are eye-catching and make great talking points with their intriguing texture and vibrant colours.

Ready to get hooked?

Alexandra Callier Taylor

Note:

The projects are graded according to how easy they are:

   * Easy

  ** Requires a little practice

*** Difficult

Contents

Equipment	6
How to crochet	8
How to knit	13

Round basket **16**   Joie-de-vivre pillow **18**   Bottle holder **20**   Esmeralda bag **22**

Table placemat **26**   Bora Bora vase **28**   Jazzy tunic **30**   Practical potholder **32**

Zen mat **34**

Seat pillow **36**

Shopping bag **40**

Cosy cat house **42**

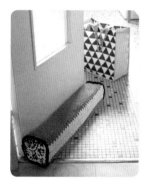

Draught excluder **44**

Exotic jewellery **46**

Laundry basket **50**

Geometric floor mat **52**

Two-colour basket **54**

Beaded door curtain **56**

Sofa pillow **58**

Lily handbag **62**

Equipment

JERSEY YARN

Jersey yarn (also known as T-shirt or fabric yarn) is a recycled yarn made from fabric offcuts from the fashion industry. The yarn varies in colour, texture and the way it hangs. This exciting fabric yarn can inspire all sorts of interesting and fun projects.

It is also used to create high-quality, stylish designs. You will be amazed by the sturdy, solid nature of your projects. The items you make will stand the test of time in the home and can more than cope with the wear and tear of family life!

CROCHET HOOKS AND KNITTING NEEDLES

All the projects have been made using a size N/15 (UK10mm) crochet hook, or size 15 (UK10mm) or size 17 (UK12mm) knitting needles.

Choose your equipment on the basis of what you are comfortable working with and how strong you need the material to be. Personally, I have worked with a bamboo crochet hook and knitting needles. If the bamboo feels a bit dry in your hands, you can oil it lightly with a bit of sweet almond oil. A good crochet hook made of wood or bamboo gets better the more you use it and improves over time.

OTHER EQUIPMENT

You will also need a sewing needle and some cotton, as well as a stitch marker for work done in the round, a cloth for the ironing stages, a pair of scissors and a tape measure for checking sizes.

How to crochet

Note on UK and US terminology: this book uses both US and UK crochet terminology; the US terms are given first, followed by the UK terms in brackets. For the US and UK term conversions, consult the chart on page 12.

HAND POSITION

The crochet hook is held between the thumb and index finger like a pen. Hold the work and the yarn in the other hand and control the yarn's tension by looping it around a finger.

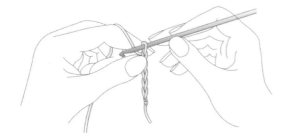

STARTING OFF: THE SLIP KNOT

This is the starting point for all crochet; it does not count as a stitch.

1. Make a loop at the end of your yarn, and hold it between thumb and middle finger.

2. Pass the hook through this loop and perform one 'yarn round hook' by hooking the yarn round the end of the crochet hook (1).

3. Pull the hooked yarn back through the loop (2).

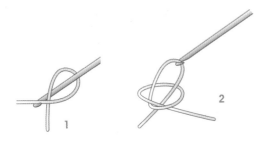

CHAIN STITCH (ch) OR TURNING STITCH

1. Yarn round hook once (1).

2. Pull the yarn through the loop that is on the crochet hook (2). You have made the first stitch.

3. Repeat this step to form a chain.

A chain is made up of chain stitches. This is generally how most projects start.

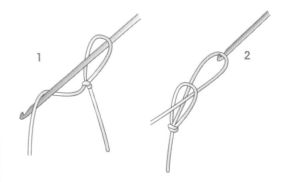

COUNTING STITCHES

All the stitches are counted as shown in the diagram. However the slip knot and the loop that are on the hook are never counted.

stitch 5
stitch 4
stitch 3
stitch 2
stitch 1

slip knot

SLIP STITCH (slst)

In this book, slip stitches are only used to join rows of projects worked in the round.

Pass the hook through the stitch where you want to do the slip stitch, yarn round hook, draw it back through the stitch and the loop that is already on the hook.

STITCH HEIGHT

So your work is even, you must always start a row with a chain stitch. As the basic stitches are different heights, adjust the number of chain stitches worked at the start of the row to match the height of the stitches in the following row. This is called a turning chain.

The table below tells you the number of chain stitches to be made before a single crochet (UK double crochet), a half-double (UK half-treble), a double (UK treble) or a treble (UK double-treble).

Number of ch required at the start of the row		
		No. of ch
1 sc (UKdc)	✕	0
1 hdc (UKhtr)	⊤	8
1 dc (UKtr)	⟊	88
1 tr (UKdtr)	⟊	888

SINGLE CROCHET (sc) / UK DOUBLE CROCHET (dc)

1. Do one chain stitch at the start of the row. This is counted as one stitch.

2. Pass the hook through the second stitch in the chain, yarn round hook, bring the loop back through, leaving 2 loops on the hook (1). Yarn round hook and draw the yarn through the 2 loops (2). This is one single crochet (UKdc).

3. For the next single crochet (UKdc), pass the hook through the next chain stitch and repeat the rest of Step 2 (3).

4. Repeat the process in each stitch to the end of the chain (4).

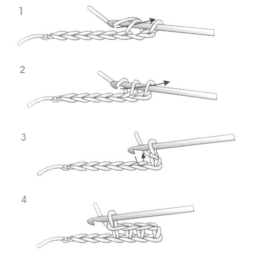

Tip

To thread jersey yarn through the eye of an embroidery needle, cut it in two lengthways for 4cm (1½in) and only thread one of the two halves through the needle.

HALF-DOUBLE (hdc) /
UK HALF-TREBLE (htr)

1. Work two chain stitches at the start of the row.
2. Yarn round hook, pass the hook through the third stitch in the chain (1), catch the yarn and draw it back through the stitch on the crochet hook, leaving three loops on the hook.
3. Yarn round hook and draw it straight through all three loops. This is one half-double (UKhtr) (2 & 3).

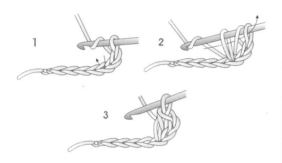

DOUBLE (dc) /
UK TREBLE (tr)

1. Work three chain stitches at the start of the row.
2. Yarn round hook, then pass the hook through the fourth stitch in the chain (1), catch the yarn and draw it back through the stitch on the crochet hook, leaving three loops on the hook.
3. Yarn round hook and draw it through the first two loops that are on the hook (2). There are now two loops on the hook.
4. Yarn round hook and draw it through the last two loops. This is a double (UKtr) (3 & 4).

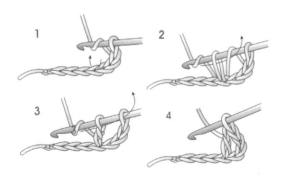

TREBLE (tr) /
UK DOUBLE-TREBLE (dtr)

1. Work four chain stitches at the start of the row.
2. Work two yarn round hooks, then pass the hook through the fifth stitch in the chain (1), catch the yarn and draw it back through the stitch on the crochet hook, leaving four loops on the hook.
3. Yarn round hook and draw it through the first two loops (2), leaving three loops on the hook.
4. Yarn round hook and draw it through the first two loops (3), leaving two loops on the hook.
5. Yarn round hook and draw it through the remaining two loops. This is a treble (UKdtr) (4 & 5).

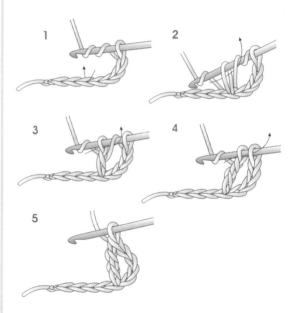

CHANGING COLOUR

If the work is being crocheted in the round: end with a slip stitch at the end of the round, cut the yarn leaving a few centimetres, then work the end of the yarn into the first stitches of the new round.

If the work is being crocheted in rows: cut the yarn leaving a few centimetres and work the strands left at the end of the row into the border stitches. Take the new yarn and, leaving a short tail, continue to crochet, keeping a tight grip on the yarn until it is securely worked into the piece. Once complete, sew the ends into the piece.

SOLOMON'S KNOT (sk)

1. Work one chain stitch. Draw out this chain stitch to get a loop around 5cm (2in) long (1).

2. Put the hook through the loop, yarn round hook; draw through the big loop. With thumb and index finger, separate the single back thread from the two front threads (2).

3. Insert the hook under the back thread, yarn round hook, drawing it back through the loop (3). You have two loops on the hook.

4. Yarn round hook and draw the new loop through the two loops on the hook. Pull tight (4). Repeat the process for each Solomon's knot.

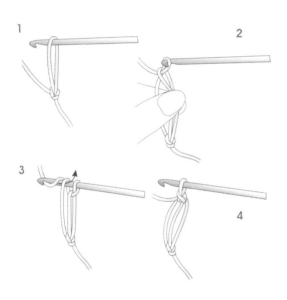

MAKING UP
With a needle

Put the two pieces side by side and sew them together with an embroidery needle, inserting it under the stitches of the left-hand and right-hand sides alternately in a zigzag.

With single crochet (UK double crochet) stitches

Place the pieces flat against each other, right sides or wrong sides facing, depending on the pattern. Use single crochet stitch (UKdc): insert the hook under the strands next to each other on the two pieces to join and work 1 sc (UKdc).

If the two pieces to join are in single crochet (UKdc) work 1 sc (UKdc) into each stitch; if they are in double crochet (UKtr), do 2 sc (UKdc) into each stitch.

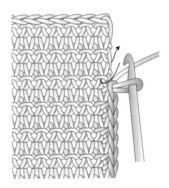

> **Tip**
> After a change of colour, work the cut yarn from the previous row into the first stitches to hide the join.

IRONING

Jersey yarn is a recycled material in which natural variations occur. You cannot create a tight lock-knit like you can with normal yarn, because this yarn is generally made up of relatively elastic jersey offcuts.

However, you can flatten the pieces and get them into shape by placing a cloth over them and giving them a hot iron. Do not hesitate to use this technique to give your piece of work the required shape and form.

READING A DIAGRAM

A diagram helps you to visualise a pattern. The stitches are represented by symbols (see the table of symbols below). Changes in colour are also shown on the diagram.

Diagrams of projects crocheted in the round are read from the inside to the outside, starting from the centre, in an anti-clockwise direction.

Diagrams of projects in rows are read from bottom to top.

12

OTHER ABBREVIATIONS

The following abbreviations are used in this book to make the instructions quicker and easier to read. You will get used to them very quickly.

Increase	inc
Decrease	dec
Right side	RS
Wrong side	WS
Stitch(es)	st(s)
Slip stitch	slst
Chain stitch, turning stitch	ch
Row	r
Repeat	rep
Next	nxt
Turn(s)	tn

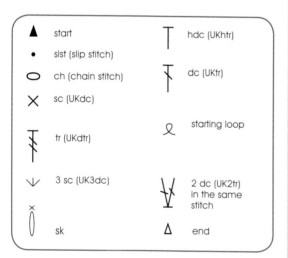

▲	start	T	hdc (UKhtr)
•	slst (slip stitch)		
○	ch (chain stitch)		dc (UKtr)
✕	sc (UKdc)		
		ℓ	starting loop
	tr (UKdtr)		
↓	3 sc (UK3dc)		2 dc (UK2tr) in the same stitch
	sk	Δ	end

How to knit

CASTING ON
(European method)

1. Take a length of yarn three times the final width of your work. Do not cut the yarn.

2. Make a slip knot near the ball on one of the needles; this forms your first stitch. Holding the needle in your right hand, rotate the slip knot under the needle so you have yarn on either side of the needle. Make a big loop with the shorter length of yarn clockwise round your left thumb and insert the needle up through this loop (1 & 2).

3. Take the longer length of yarn that you have in your right hand around the needle, slip the loop over the point of the needle and let it slide off the thumb when it is on the other side of the needle. Pull the yarn to tighten slightly.

4. Repeat this step to form the number of stitches as instructed in the pattern.

GARTER STITCH
The yarn is at the back of the work, on the left-hand side and you are working with the ball end placed round your right index finger.

1. Insert the right-hand needle up through the first stitch, behind the left-hand needle, taking the yarn under the right-hand needle (1).

2. Wrap the yarn from back to front over the right-hand needle (2).

3. Take the right-hand needle back through the stitch so that you pick up the yarn that you have just wrapped round and the needle is sitting in front of the left-hand needle. This makes a loop that will create the new stitch (3).

4. Slide the stitch off the left-hand needle; you have formed a new stitch (4).

5. Repeat the process with the other stitches until all the stitches have passed onto the right-hand needle; you now have another row (5).

13

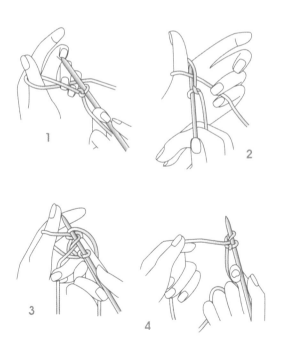

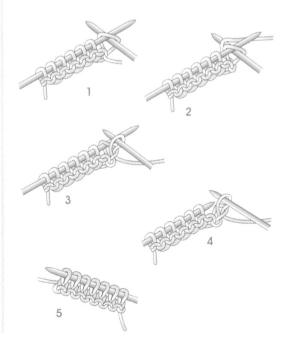

PURL STITCH

The yarn is kept at the front of the work.

1. Insert the right-hand needle through the first stitch, in front of the left-hand needle, keeping the yarn at the front (1).

2. Wrap the yarn from back to front over the right-hand needle (2).

3. Slide the right-hand needle back under the left-hand needle so that you pick up the yarn that you have just wrapped round. This makes a loop that will create the new stitch (3).

4. Slide the stitch off the left-hand needle; you have formed a new stitch (4).

5. Repeat the process with the other stitches, until all the stitches have passed onto the right-hand needle; you have got another row (5).

STOCKING STITCH

Odd rows: On the right side of the work, knit all the stitches.

Even rows: On the wrong side of the work, purl all the stitches.

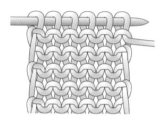

SLIPPED STITCH

The slipped stitch is a stitch from the lower row passed directly onto the right-hand needle.

Put the yarn to the front or back of the work, according to the instructions, insert the right-hand needle into the stitch on the left-hand needle as though you are going to do a knit stitch and slide it directly onto the right-hand needle without working it.

> **Tip**
>
> *Once you have finished a row, swap the needles to the opposite hands, turning the work as you do, so that the complete work always starts in your left hand and you are sliding the stitches over to the right-hand needle.*

SELVEDGE STITCH

The selvedge stitch is the first or last stitch of each row. It is done in knit stitch on the rows on the right side and purl stitch on the rows on the wrong side. There is therefore a selvedge on both edges of your work. Selvedge stitches are for assembling the different parts of the work: you sew through the selvedge when you put the pieces together.

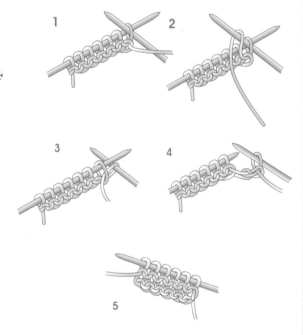

14

CROSSED STITCH

Crossed stitch is worked with 2 colours, over 8 rows. It starts on the wrong side of the work.

Row 1, crossed stitch colour: 1 selvedge st, sl1 with yarn in back, *sl2 with yarn in back, p1, sl3 with yarn in back*. Rep from * to *. Finish with 1 selvedge stitch.

Rows 2 and 6, background colour: purl.

Rows 3 and 7, background colour: knit.

Row 4, cross stitch colour: 1 selvedge st, *p1 taking into the stitch the yarn from Row 1, sl5 with yarn in back*. Rep from * to *. P1, taking into the stitch the yarn from Row 1, 1 selvedge st.

Row 5, crossed stitch colour: 1 selvedge st, sl1 with yarn in front, *sl5 with yarn in back, sl1 with yarn in front*. Rep from * to *. Finish with 1 selvedge st.

Row 8, crossed stitch colour: 1 selvedge st, *sl3 with yarn in back, p1 taking into the st the yarn from Row 5, sl2 with yarn in back*. Rep from * to *. Sl1 with yarn in back, 1 selvedge st.

Rep these 8 rows.

15

CASTING OFF

Cast off to finish the work.

1. Knit the first 2 stitches, draw the first stitch over the second and let it slip off the needle (1).

You have one stitch left on the needle.

2. Knit the following stitch and repeat the process until the end of the row (2). You then have only one stitch on the needle: cut the yarn, thread it through the loop and pull gently to close.

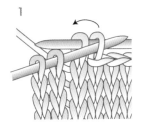

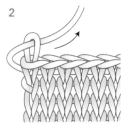

Round basket ✳✳

A beautifully shaped basket inspired by the markets of Central America, revisited with a graphic, urban twist.

MATERIALS

✳ Jersey yarn (medium thickness): 1½ balls of taupe plus remnants of red
✳ N/15 (10mm) crochet hook
✳ Large embroidery needle

TECHNIQUE USED

Crochet

STITCHES USED

✳ Chain stitch (ch)
✳ Slip stitch (slst)
✳ Single crochet (sc)/ UK double crochet (UKdc)

THE BASKET

With taupe yarn, make 4 ch, join with a slst to form the starting ring.

Round 1: 1 ch, 9 sc (UKdc) into the starting ring. You have 9 sts. End the round with 1 slst.

Round 2: 1 ch, 2 sc (UKdc) into each st of previous round. You have 18 sts. End the round with 1 slst.

Round 3: 1 ch, 1 sc (UKdc) into each st of previous round. You have 18 sts. End the round with 1 slst.

Round 4: 1 ch, *1 sc (UKdc) into each of the first 2 sts, 2 sc (UKdc) into following st.* Rep 6 times from * to *. You have 24 sts. End the round with 1 slst.

Round 5: 1 ch, *1 sc (UKdc) into each of the first 3 sts, 2 sc (UKdc) into following st.* Rep 6 times from * to *. You have 30 sts. End the round with 1 slst.

Round 6: 1 ch, *1 sc (UKdc) into each of the first 4 sts, 2 sc (UKdc) into following st.* Rep 6 times from * to *. You have 36 sts. End the round with 1 slst.

Round 7: 1 ch, *1 sc (UKdc) into each of the first 5 sts, 2 sc (UKdc) into following st.* Rep 6 times from * to *. You have 42 sts. End the round with 1 slst.

Round 8: 1 ch, *1 sc (UKdc) into each of the first 6 sts, 2 sc (UKdc) into following st.* Rep 6 times from * to *. You have 48 sts. End the round with 1 slst.

Round 9: 1 ch, *1 sc (UKdc) into each of the first 7 sts, 2 sc (UKdc) into following st.* Rep 6 times from * to *. You have 54 sts. End the round with 1 slst.

Round 10: 1 ch, *1 sc (UKdc) into each of the first 8 sts, 2 sc (UKdc) into following st.* Rep 6 times from * to *. You have 60 sts. End the round with 1 slst.

Rounds 11 to 16: 1 ch, 1 sc (UKdc) into each st of previous round. You have 60 sts on each round. End each round with 1 slst.

Round 17: 1 ch, *1 sc (UKdc) into each of the first 8 sts, 1 dec.* Rep 6 times from * to *. You have 54 sts. End the round with 1 slst.

Round 18: 1 ch, *1 sc (UKdc) into each of the first 7 sts, 1 dec.* Rep 6 times from * to *. You have 48 sts. End the round with 1 slst.

Round 19: 1 ch, *1 sc (UKdc) into each of the first 6 sts, 1 dec.* Rep 6 times from * to *. You have 42 sts. End the round with 1 slst.

Round 20: 1 ch, *1 sc (UKdc) into each of the first 5 sts, 1 dec.* Rep 6 times from * to.* You have 36 sts. End the round with 1 slst. Fasten off.

THE MOTIFS

Using red yarn, make six motifs.

For each motif: 5 ch, join with a slst to form the starting ring. 1 ch, then 10 sc (UKdc) into the ring.

End each motif with a slst. Cut the yarn, leaving around 10cm (4in).

MAKING UP

1. Using an embroidery needle, attach the six red motifs to the rim of the basket at regular intervals: make a solid knot with the surplus yarn round the outside strand of the basket's single (UKdouble) crochet stitches.

2. Sew in any remaining ends of yarn.

Joie-de-vivre pillow *

A vibrant pillow to give your favourite armchair a festive feel.

MATERIALS

* Jersey yarn (average thickness): remnants in sky blue, navy blue, royal blue, orange, pink, red and taupe
* N/15 (10mm) crochet hook
* Large embroidery needle
* Square cushion slip, 45cm (17½in) each side

TECHNIQUE USED
Crochet

STITCHES USED

* Double crochet (dc)/ UK treble (tr)
* Half-double (hdc)/ UK half-treble (htr)
* Slip stitch (slst)
* Chain stitch (ch)
* Single crochet (sc) UK double (dc)

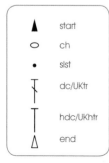

▲	start
○	ch
•	slst
⊤	dc/UKtr
⊤	hdc/UKhtr
△	end

The pillow is made up of nine separate squares, so you need to follow the diagram below nine times using different colours: 1 taupe/orange square, 1 taupe/royal blue square, 1 sky blue/pink square, 1 taupe/navy blue square, 1 orange/pink square, 2 taupe/red squares, 1 sky blue/taupe square, 1 royal blue/sky blue square.

THE SQUARE
With the first colour, make 4 ch, join with a slst to form the starting ring.

Round 1: 3 ch, 2 dc (UKtr) into the starting ring, 2 ch, 3 dc (UKtr) into the starting ring, 1 ch. Continue with the second colour: 1 ch, 3 dc (UKtr) into the starting ring, 2 ch, 3 dc (UKtr) into the starting ring, 1 ch. End with 1 hdc (UKhtr) into the 3rd ch from the start of the round. Turn the work over.

Round 2: 3 ch, 2 dc (UKtr) into the space made by the hdc (UKhtr) at the end of Round 1, 1 ch, 3 dc (UKtr) into the 2 ch forming the next corner of Round 1, 2 ch, 3 dc (UKtr) into the 2 ch of the same corner, 1 ch, 3 dc (UKtr) into the 2 ch forming the next corner of Round 1, 1 ch. Change to the first colour: 1 ch, 3 dc (UKtr) into the 2 ch of the same corner, 1 ch, 3 dc (UKtr) into the 2 ch forming the next corner of Round 1, 2 ch, 3 dc (UKtr) into the 2 ch of the same corner, 1 ch, 3 dc (UKtr), 1 ch. End with 1 hdc (UKhtr) into the third ch from the start of the round.
Cut the yarn and fasten off.
Make the other eight squares in the same way.

MAKING UP
1. Flatten out the squares, place a cloth on top and iron them into shape.
2. With the orange yarn, join the squares into rows of three: place them wrong sides facing and work a round of sc (UKdc), ensuring you have the diagonal stripes from the colour changes going in the same direction. You will now have three rows of three squares.
3. Join the rows together, by placing them wrong sides facing and with orange yarn, work a round of sc (UKdc).
4. With navy blue, make a border of 2 rows of sc (UKdc), working 3 sc (UKdc) at the corners to give them a good shape.
You end up with a square measuring around 45cm (17½in) along each side.
5. With an embroidery needle and thread, use secure slip stitches through the pillow slip to attach the pillow cover.

Tip
You can make the cushion slip yourself rather than buying one.

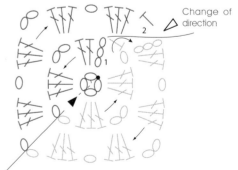

Change of direction

Colour change

Bottle holder **

A practical way to keep your drinks to hand during a family meal or dinner with friends.

MATERIALS

❋ Jersey yarn (medium thickness): 1 ball of taupe and some remnants of fuchsia
❋ N/15 (10mm) crochet hook
❋ Round handle

TECHNIQUE USED

Crochet

STITCHES USED

❋ Double crochet (dc)/ UK treble (tr)
❋ Slip stitch (slst)
❋ Chain stitch (ch)
❋ Single crochet (sc)/ UK double crochet (dc)

THE CYLINDER

With the fuchsia yarn, make 5 ch, join with a slst to form the starting ring.

Round 1: 3 ch, 15 dc (UKtr) into the starting ring. End the round with 1 slst into the third ch.

Rounds 2 and 3: 3 ch, 15 dc (UKtr). End the round with 1 slst into the third ch. Cut the yarn.

Rounds 4 to 7: with the taupe yarn, 3 ch, 15 dc (UKtr). End the round with 1 slst into the third ch.

Fasten off and cut the yarn leaving around 10cm (4in), but do not work in.

Make the other three cylinders in the same way.

MAKING UP

1. Make a solid knot in the four strands left at the end of the work on each cylinder.
2. Pull two strands to the left and two to the right; they will be worked in when the handle is attached.
3. Attach the cylinders together around the assembly knot with a round of sc (UKdc) (see page 11): two cylinders to the right of the knot and two cylinders to the left of the knot.

Round 8: Count 4 sts from the knot between the four cylinders. With the taupe yarn, work 2 sc (UKdc) into each of the first 4 sts after the assembly knot, attaching the first two cylinders together. You have done 8 sc (UKdc) and come back to the assembly knot.

On the other side of the knot, work 2 sc (UKdc) into each of the first 4 sts after the knot to attach the other two cylinders. You have 8 sc (UKdc) on either side of the starting knot (16 sc (UKdc) in total). You are 8 sc (UKdc) from the starting assembly knot of the four cylinders and 16 sc (UKdc) from the beginning of the round. The cylinders are assembled two by two on either side of the starting knot.

Round 9: Turn the work round. 1 ch, 4 sc (UKdc). Attach the handle and crochet the yarn around it: 1 sc (UKdc) into each of the next 3 sts, 2 sc (UKdc) into each of the next 2 sts, then 1 sc (UKdc) into each of the next 3 sts. You have 10 sc (UKdc) on the handle, including 4 sc (UKdc) in the centre that conceal the starting knot.

Finish with 4 sc (UKdc) in each of the last 4 sts of Round 8. Cut the yarn and fasten off.

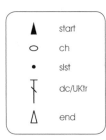

▲	start
○	ch
•	slst
⊤	dc/UKtr
△	end

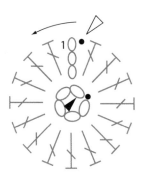

Esmeralda bag ✳✳✳

A feminine, drum-shaped handbag to glam up your evening outfit.

MATERIALS

✳ Jersey yarn (medium
   thickness): ¼ of a
   ball each of royal
   blue, fuchsia, light
   grey and red
✳ N/15 (10mm)
   crochet hook
✳ size 17 (12mm)
   knitting needles
✳ Embroidery needle
✳ Bamboo handles
✳ Polyester interfacing:
   20 x 45cm (8 x 18in)
✳ Sewing thread

TECHNIQUE USED
Crochet and knitting

STITCHES USED
✳ Double crochet (dc)/
   UK treble (tr)
✳ Slip stitch (slst)
✳ Chain stitch (ch)
✳ Single crochet (sc)/
   UK double crochet
   (dc)
✳ Crossed stitch

THE MAIN PANEL

Knitted in crossed stitch, with royal blue yarn for the background and red for the crosses.

1. Cast on 39 sts on your knitting needle.
2. Knit crossed stitch for 20 rows (see page 15). Note that the stitch begins on the wrong side of the work. As the pattern repeats every 8 rows, you get two and a half pattern repeats.
3. Row 21: purl.
Cast off the stitches and cut the yarn.
4. Make the border: using the red yarn and your crochet hook, work a row of sc (UKdc) around the panel, working 3 sc (UKdc) into each of the corner stitches to form neat right-angles.
5. With the fuchsia yarn: work a second row of sc (UKdc), working 3 sc (UKdc) into the corners.
6. Using a cloth, flatten and shape the panel with a hot iron. You should have a panel of around 20 x 45cm (8 x 18in) inside the borders.
7. Using invisible stitches, sew the piece of interfacing onto the back of the panel, making sure you don't overlap onto the crocheted border.

THE OPENING

1. Fold the panel, wrong sides facing, to form a cylinder.
2. Join the ends of the short sides of the panel: from each corner, using fuchsia yarn, work 5 sc (UKdc), taking the border on either side into the row. Cut and fasten off the yarn. The free stitches in the middle are where the handles will be.

THE SIDES OF THE BAG

1. With the fuchsia yarn, work 1 round of dc (UKtr) at each end of the cylinder: 3 ch, 1 dc (UKtr) into every stitch all round the cylinder. End with 1 slst into the third ch from the start of the round. Cut the yarn and fasten off.

2. Make 2 rounds of dc (UKtr) to close the ends of the cylinder: with grey yarn, make 5 ch, join with 1 slst to form the starting ring.

Round 1: 3 ch, 15 dc (UKtr) into the starting ring. End with 1 slst into the third ch from the start of the round.

Round 2: 3 ch, 1 dc (UKtr) into the same place. 2 dc (UKtr) into each dc (UKtr) of the previous round. End with 1 slst into the third ch from the start of the round. You have 31 dc (UKtr).

3. Join the rounds of dc (UKtr), wrong sides facing, to the fuchsia dc (UKtr) rounds, by doing a round of sc (UKdc) through the back strand at the top of the dc (UKtr) stitches. End with 1 slst.

Cut the yarn and fasten off. The body of the bag is finished.

THE HANDLES

1. With the fuchsia yarn, work 1 row of sc (UKdc) through the free stitches either side of the opening in the centre of the cylinder, crocheting the yarn round each handle.

2. Cut the yarn and fasten off.

▲	start
○	ch
•	slst
⊤	dc/UKtr
⋎	2 dc (UK2tr) in the same st
△	end

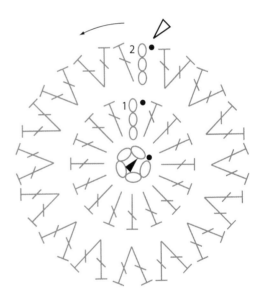

25

Table placemat *

An eye-catching placemat to bring colour to your meals.

MATERIALS

✳ Jersey yarn (average
  thickness): remnants in
  navy blue, fuchsia
  and taupe
✳ N/15 (10mm)
  crochet hook

TECHNIQUE USED
Crochet

STITCHES USED
✳ Double crochet (dc)/
  UK treble (tr)
✳ Slip stitch (slst)
✳ Chain stitch (ch)

With the blue yarn, make 8 ch, then work 5 ch to start the rectangle.

Round 1: 2 dc (UKtr) into the sixth ch from hook, 1 dc (UKtr) into each ch until the second-to-last ch of the foundation chain. Into the last ch: 2 dc (UKtr), 2 ch, 3 dc (UKtr), 2 ch, 2 dc (UKtr). On the other side of the foundation chain: 1 dc (UKtr) into each ch until the starting ch. Into this ch, which already contains 2 dc (UKtr) that you've done previously: 2 dc (UKtr), 2 ch, 2 dc (UKtr).
End with 1 slst into the third ch of the 5 ch.
Round 2: 1 slst into the fourth ch of the previous round's 5 ch. 5 ch to start Round 2. 2 dc (UKtr) into the fifth ch of the previous round's 5 ch, 1 dc (UKtr) into each stitch. Continue until the corner space formed in the previous round by 2 ch.

In this space: *2 dc (UKtr), 2 ch, 2 dc (UKtr)*, 1 dc (UKtr) into each of the next dc (UKtr) of the previous round: you get to the second corner and you have made a long side and a short side of the rectangle. Rep from * to * , putting the hook through the corner space then 1 dc (UKtr) into each dc (UKtr) of the previous round until the next corner: you are on the third corner.
Rep from * to *. Continue with 1 dc (UKtr) into each dc (UKtr) of the previous round.
End with 1 slst into the third ch of the 5 ch at the start of Round 2.
Rep the process for the remaining rounds, working 2 rounds in fuchsia and 1 round in taupe to finish.
On each turn, you have an inc of 4 dc (UKtr) on each side of the rectangle. End the last round with 1 slst, cut the yarn and fasten off. Press the rectangle with a hot iron using a cloth.

26

▲	start
○	ch
•	slst
⊤	dc/UKtr
V	2 dc (UK2tr) in the same st
△	end

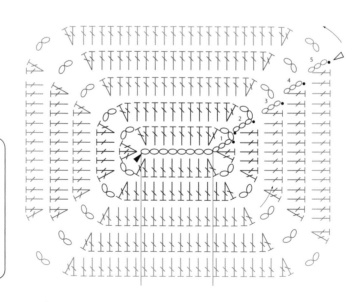

Bora Bora vase **

The tropical colours of this original vase will transport you to a lagoon-side cabana.

MATERIALS

❋ Jersey yarn (bulky thickness): ½ a ball each of dark grey and yellow, ¼ of a ball of royal blue and remnants of turquoise yarn

❋ N/15 (10mm) crochet hook

TECHNIQUE USED

Crochet

STITCHES USED

❋ Slip stitch (slst)

❋ Chain stitch (ch)

❋ Single crochet (sc)/ UK double crochet (dc)

With the grey yarn, make 4 ch, join with a slst to form the starting ring.

Round 1: 1 ch, 9 sc (UKdc) into the starting ring. You have 9 sts. End the round with 1 slst.

Round 2: 1 ch, 2 sc (UKdc) into each st of previous round. You have 18 sts. End the round with 1 slst.

Round 3: 1 ch, 1 sc (UKdc) into each st of previous round. You have 18 sts. End the round with 1 slst.

Round 4: 1 ch, *1 sc (UKdc) into each of the first 2 sts, 2 sc (UKdc) into following st.* Rep 6 times from * to *. You have 24 sts. End the round with 1 slst.

Round 5: 1 ch, *1 sc (UKdc) into each of the first 3 sts, 2 sc (UKdc) into following st.* Rep 6 times from * to *. You have 30 sts. End the round with 1 slst.

Round 6: 1 ch, *1 sc (UKdc) into each of the first 4 sts, 2 sc (UKdc) into following st.* Rep 6 times from * to *. You have 36 sts. End the round with 1 slst.

Round 7: 1 ch, *1 sc (UKdc) into each of the first 5 sts, 2 sc (UKdc) into following st.* Rep 6 times from * to *. You have 42 sts. End the round with 1 slst.

Round 8: 1 ch, *1 sc (UKdc) into each of the first 6 sts, 2 sc (UKdc) into following st.* Rep 6 times from * to *. You have 48 sts. End the round with 1 slst.

Round 9, with royal blue yarn: 1 ch, *1 sc (UKdc) into each of the first 7 sts, 2 sc (UKdc) into following st.* Rep 6 times from * to *. You have 54 sts. End the round with 1 slst.

Round 10: 1 ch, *1 sc (UKdc) into each of the first 8 sts, 2 sc (UKdc) into following st.* Rep 6 times from * to *. You have 60 sts. End the round with 1 slst.

Round 11, with the yellow yarn: 1 ch, *1 sc (UKdc) into each of the first 9 sts, 2 sc

(UKdc) into following st.* Rep 6 times from * to .* You have 66 sts. End the round with 1 slst.

Round 12: 1 ch, *1 sc (UKdc) into each of the first 10 sts, 2 sc (UKdc) into following st.* Rep 6 times from * to *. You have 72 sts. End the round with 1 slst.

Rounds 13 and 14: with turquoise yarn: 1 ch, *1 sc (UKdc) into each of the first 10 sts, 2 sc (UKdc) into following st.* Rep 6 times from * to *. You have 72 sts. End the round with 1 slst.

Round 15: with grey yarn: 1 ch, *1 sc (UKdc) into each of the first 9 sts, 2 sc (UKdc) into following st.* Rep 6 times from * to.* You have 66 sts. End the round with 1 slst.

Round 16: 1 ch, *1 sc (UKdc) into each of the first 8 sts, 2 sc (UKdc) into following st.* Rep 6 times from * to *. You have 60 sts. End the round with 1 slst.

Round 17: 1 ch, *1 sc (UKdc) into each of the first 7 sts, 2 sc (UKdc) into following st.* Rep 6 times from * to *. You have 54 sts. End the round with 1 slst.

Round 18: 1 ch, * 1 sc (UKdc) into each of the first 6 sts, 2 sc (UKdc) into following st.* Rep 6 times from * to *. You have 48 sts. End the round with 1 slst.

Round 19: with royal blue yarn: 1 ch, *1 sc (UKdc) into each of the first 5 sts, 2 sc (UKdc) into following st.* Rep 6 times from * to.* You have 42 sts. End the round with 1 slst.

Round 20: 1 ch, *1 sc (UKdc) into each of the first 4 sts, 2 sc (UKdc) into following st.* Rep 6 times from * to.* You have 36 sts. End the round with 1 slst.

Rounds 21 to 26: with yellow yarn: 1 ch, 35 sc (UKdc). You have 36 sts. End the round with 1 slst.

Rounds 27 and 28: with grey yarn: 1 ch, 35 sc (UKdc). You have 36 sts. End the round with 1 slst.

Cut the yarn and fasten off.

Jazzy tunic **

Inspired by the golden voices of jazz, this contrasting openwork piece will charm your fans.

MATERIALS

❋ Jersey yarn
   (medium thickness):
   1 ball of black
❋ N/15 (10mm)
   crochet hook
❋ 1 fabric flower

TECHNIQUE USED
Crochet

STITCHES USED
❋ Double crochet (dc)/
   UK treble (tr)
❋ Slip stitch (slst)
❋ Chain stitch (ch)
❋ Single crochet (sc)/
   UK double crochet
   (dc)
❋ Solomon's knot (sk)

THE BODY OF THE TUNIC

This tunic is made using Solomon's knots (see page 11). To get an attractive result, space the Solomon's knots at regular intervals, crocheting them 5cm (2in) apart.

Row 1: 63 ch, end with 1 slst.
Row 2: 3 ch, 62 dc (UKtr), end with 1 slst.
Row 3: 1 sc (UKdc), 1 sk, 1 sk attached to the strip of dc (UKtr) by 1 sc (UKdc) in the seventh dc (UKtr) after the sc (UKdc) at the start of the row, *1 sk, 1 sk attached to the strip of dc (UKtr) by 1 sc (UKdc) in the seventh dc (UKtr) after the last sk attached to the dc (UKtr).* Rep 5 times from * to *. You have reached the 56th dc (UKtr). 1 sk, 1 sk attached to the sc (UKdc) at the start of the row by 1 new sc (UKdc).
Row 4: 2 sk, 1 sk attached to the first sk of the previous row by 1 sc (UKdc), 1 sk, *1 sk attached to the next sk by 1 sc (UKdc), 1 sk*. Rep 5 times from * to *. 1 sk attached to the following sk by 1 sc (UKdc), 1 sk attached to the second sk from the start of the row by 1 sc (UKdc).

Following odd rows: *1 sk, 1 sk attached to the next sk by 1 sc (UKdc)*. Rep 6 times from * to *.
1 sk, 1 sk attached to the sk at the start of the row by 1 sc (UKdc).
Following even rows: 2 sk, *1 sk attached to the next sk by 1 sc (UKdc), 1 sk.* Rep 6 times from * to *.
1 sk attached to the next sk from the previous row by 1 sc (UKdc), 1 sk attached to the second sk from the start of the row by 1 sc (UKdc).
Work a minimum of 6 rows. Carry on crocheting if you want the garment to be longer in the body.

THE SHOULDER STRAPS

1. Make the first shoulder strap: *1 sc (UKdc) into the strip of dc (UKtr), 20 ch, 1 sc (UKdc) into the sixteenth dc (UKtr) from the dc (UKtr) where you started the shoulder strap*. Cut and fasten off.
2. For the other strap, repeat from * to * starting from the sixteenth dc (UKtr) along. Cut and fasten off.

▲	start	
○	ch	
×	sc/UKdc	
⊤	dc/UKtr	
×	sk	

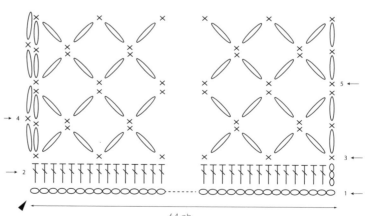

64 ch

Practical potholder *

A modern reinterpretation of an easy-to-make basic design.

MATERIAL
❋ Jersey yarn (bulky
  thickness): remnants
  of dark grey
❋ Jersey yarn (medium
  thickness): remnants
  of orange
❋ N/15 (10mm)
  crochet hook

TECHNIQUE USED
Crochet

STITCHES USED
❋ Double crochet (dc)/
  UK treble (tr)
❋ Slip stitch (slst)
❋ Chain stitch (ch)
❋ Single crochet (sc)/
  UK double crochet
  (dc)

THE POTHOLDER
Crocheted in rows.
Make a loop with the grey yarn.

Row 1: 3 ch, 1 dc (UKtr), 3 ch and 2 dc (UKtr) into the starting loop. Turn the work over.

Row 2: 3 ch, 1 dc (UKtr), *2 dc (UKtr), 3 ch, 2 dc (UKtr).* From * to * stitch the dc (UKtr) into the corner space formed by the ch of the previous row. 2 dc (UKtr), with the last one crocheted into the third ch of the selvedge of Row 1. Turn the work over.

Row 3: 3 ch, 3 dc (UKtr), *2 dc (UKtr), 3 ch, 2 dc (UKtr).* From * to * stitch the dc (UKtr) into the corner space formed by the ch of the previous row. 4 dc (UKtr), with the last one crocheted into the third ch of the selvedge of Row 2. Turn the work over.

Row 4: 3 ch, 5 dc (UKtr), *2 dc (UKtr), 3 ch, 2 dc (UKtr).* From * to * stitch the dc (UKtr) into the corner space formed by the ch of the previous row. 6 dc (UKtr), the last crocheted into the third ch of the selvedge of Row 3.
To finish, cut the yarn and fasten off.

Flatten out the square and iron it into shape using a cloth. Allow to dry.

THE BORDER
1. With the orange yarn: 1 sc (UKdc) into a corner, 10 ch. Close the loop with 1 sc (UKdc) to form the ring the potholder will hang from.
2. Continue with a border of sc (UKdc) all around the square. Finish with 1 slst, cut the yarn and fasten off.

> **Tip**
> Use a colour that won't show the dirt for the main square and give your potholder a nice bright border so it is easy to find in the kitchen.

▲	start
℺	starting ring
○	ch
⊤	dc/UKtr
△	end

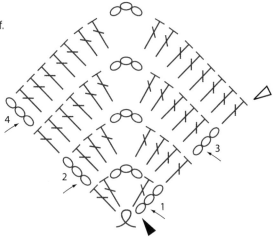

Zen mat **

A minimalist mat with elegant details that catches the light.

MATERIALS

❉ Jersey yarn (medium thickness): ½ ball of beige and 4 balls of black

❉ N/15 (10mm) crochet hook

❉ Stitch marker

TECHNIQUE USED

Crochet

STITCHES USED

❉ Double crochet (dc)/ UK treble (tr)

❉ Slip stitch (slst)

❉ Chain stitch (ch)

❉ Single crochet (sc)/ UK dc

▲	start
○	ch
•	slst
×	sc/UKdc
⋁	3 sc/UK3dc

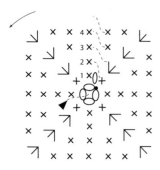

The mat consists of six squares: you need to follow the diagram six times. Always use a stitch marker to identify the last stitch of the row.

A SQUARE

With the beige yarn, make 4 ch, join with a slst to form a small starting ring.

Round 1: 1 ch, 8 sc (UKdc) into the starting ring.

Round 2: *1 sc (UKdc) into the next sc (UKdc), 3 sc (UKdc) into the next sc (UKdc).* Rep 3 times from * to *.

Round 3: *1 sc (UKdc) into each of the next 2 sc (UKdc), 3 sc (UKdc) into the next st, 1 sc (UKdc) into the next st.* Rep 3 times from * to *.

Round 4: *1 sc (UKdc) into each of the next 3 sc (UKdc), 3 sc (UKdc) into the next sc (UKdc), 1 sc (UKdc) into each of the next 2 sc (UKdc).* Rep 3 times from * to *.

Round 5: *1 sc (UKdc) into each of the next 4 sc (UKdc), 3 sc (UKdc) into the next sc (UKdc), 1 sc (UKdc) into each of the next 3 sc (UKdc).* Rep 3 times from * to *.

Round 6: *1 sc (UKdc) into each of the next 5 sc (UKdc), 3 sc (UKdc) into the next sc (UKdc), 1 sc (UKdc) into each of the next 4 sc (UKdc).* Rep 3 times from * to *.

Round 7: *1 sc (UKdc) into each of the next 6 sc (UKdc), 3 sc (UKdc) into the next sc (UKdc), 1 sc (UKdc) into each of the next 5 sc (UKdc).* Rep 3 times from * to *.

Round 8: *1 sc (UKdc) into each of the next 7 sc (UKdc), 3 sc (UKdc) into the next sc (UKdc), 1 sc (UKdc) into each of the next 6 sc (UKdc).* Rep 3 times from * to *.

Round 9: *1 sc (UKdc) into each of the next 8 sc (UKdc), 3 sc (UKdc) into the next sc (UKdc), 1 sc (UKdc) into each of the next 7 sc (UKdc).* Rep 3 times from * to *.

Round 10: *1 sc (UKdc) into each of the next 9 sc (UKdc), 3 sc (UKdc) into the next sc (UKdc), 1 sc (UKdc) into each of the next 8 sc (UKdc).* Rep 3 times from * to *.

Round 11: *1 sc (UKdc) into each of the next 10 sc (UKdc), 3 sc (UKdc) into the next sc (UKdc), 1 sc (UKdc) into each of the next 9 sc (UKdc).* Rep 3 times from * to *.

Round 12: *1 sc (UKdc) into each of the next 11 sc (UKdc), 3 sc (UKdc) into the next sc (UKdc), 1 sc (UKdc) into each of the next 10 sc (UKdc).* Rep 3 times from * to *.

Fasten off and cut the yarn. Make the other five squares in the same way.

MAKING UP

1. Flatten out the squares and iron them carefully using a cloth.

2. With the beige yarn: assemble the squares into strips of three, right sides together, join using 1 round of sc (UKdc). You now have 2 strips of 3 squares.

3. With the beige yarn: assemble these two strips, right sides together, using 1 round of sc (UKdc) along the full length. As you are putting the two strips together, work the yarn from the squares into the sc (UKdc) to give a perfect finish.

The rounds of assembly sc (UKdc) will end up underneath the mat.

4. With the black yarn: make a border of dc (UKtr) all around the outside, ensuring the corners are well formed: do 2 dc (UKtr), 2 ch, 2 dc (UKtr) into each corner stitch. Cut and fasten off the yarn.

5. Using a cloth, press the mat with a hot iron to flatten it out.

Seat pillow **

Pretty pillows to give a touch of colourful comfort to your chairs, or to take with you on a picnic.

MATERIALS

❋ *Jersey yarn (medium thickness): 1/3 ball each of China blue, light grey and red*

❋ *N/15 (10mm) crochet hook*

TECHNIQUE USED

Crochet

STITCHES USED

❋ *Double crochet (dc)/ UK treble (tr)*

❋ *Treble crochet (tr)/ UK double-treble (dtr)*

❋ *Slip stitch (slst)*

❋ *Chain stitch (ch)*

❋ *Single crochet (sc)/ UK double crochet (dc)*

Tip

The yarn from each colour change can be worked into the first stitches of the next round to give a perfect finish.

THE BLUE AND RED COVER

With red yarn: make 4 ch, join with a slst to form the starting ring.

Round 1: 3 ch, 11 dc (UKtr) into the starting ring. End with 1 slst into the third ch from the start of the round. Cut the yarn.

Round 2: with grey yarn: 3 ch, 2 dc (UKtr) into each dc (UKtr) of Round 1. End with 1 slst into the third ch from the start of the round. Cut the yarn.

Round 3: with China blue yarn: 3 ch, *2 dc (UKtr) into the next st, 1 dc (UKtr), 1 tr (UKdtr) into the same place hooked through Round 1.* Rep from * to * to the end of the round. End with 1 slst into the third ch from the start of the round. Cut the yarn.

Round 4: with red yarn: 1 ch, 1 round of sc (UKdc). End with 1 slst into the third ch from the start of the round. Cut the yarn.

Round 5: with grey yarn: 3 ch, *2 dc (UKtr) into the next stitch, 1 dc (UKtr), 1 dc (UKtr).* Rep from * to * to the end of the round. End with 1 slst into the third ch from the start of the round. Cut the yarn.

Round 6: with China blue yarn: 3 ch, *2 dc (UKtr) into the next st, 1 dc (UKtr), 1 tr (UKdtr) into the same place hooked through round 4*. Rep from * to * until the end of the round. End with 1 slst into the third ch from the start of the round. Cut the yarn.

Round 7: with red yarn: 1 ch, 1 round of sc (UKdc). End with 1 slst into the third ch from the start. Cut the yarn and fasten off.

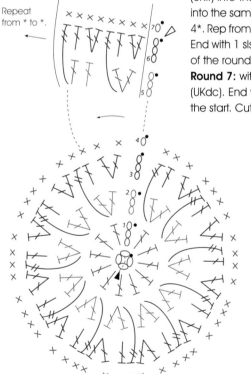

Repeat from * to *.

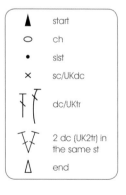

▲	start
○	ch
•	slst
×	sc/UKdc
⊤⊤	dc/UKtr
V	2 dc (UK2tr) in the same st
△	end

MATERIALS

❉ *Jersey yarn (medium thickness): Remnants of sky blue, navy blue, light grey, orange and pink*

❉ *N/15 (10mm) crochet hook*

TECHNIQUE USED

Crochet

STITCHED USED

❉ *Double crochet (dc)/ UK treble (tr)*

❉ *Slip stitch (slst)*

❉ *Chain stitch (ch)*

❉ *Single crochet (sc)/ UK double crochet (dc)*

THE ORANGE AND PINK COVER

With sky blue yarn: make 4 ch, join with a slst to form the starting ring.

Round 1: 3 ch, 15 dc (UKtr) through the starting ring, end with 1 slst into the third ch from the start of the round. Cut the yarn.

Round 2: with grey yarn: 3 ch, 2 dc (UKtr) into each dc (UKtr) of round 1. End with 1 slst into the third ch from the start of the round. Cut the yarn.

Round 3: with navy blue yarn: 3 ch, *2 dc (UKtr) into the next stitch, 1 dc (UKtr).* Rep from * to * to the end of the round. End with 1 slst into the third ch from the start of the round. Cut the yarn.

Round 4: with pink yarn: 1 ch, *3 sc (UKdc), 1 dc (UKtr) in the same place hooked into Round 2.* Rep from * to * to the end of the round. End with 1 slst into the third ch from the start. Cut the yarn.

Round 5: with sky blue yarn: 3 ch, *3 dc (UKtr), 2 dc (UKtr) sewn into the same st.* Rep from * to * to the end of the round. End with 1 slst into the third ch from the start of the round. Cut the yarn.

Round 6: with grey yarn: 3 ch, *4 dc (UKtr), 2 dc (UKtr) sewn into the same st.* Rep from * to * to the end of the round. End with 1 slst into the third ch from the start of the round. Cut the yarn.

Round 7: with orange yarn: 1 ch, *3 sc (UKdc), 1 dc (UKtr) hooked into Round 5.* Rep from * to * to the end of the round. End with 1 slst into the third ch from the start. Cut the yarn and fasten off.

With orange yarn, make a chain worked into the top of Round 1.

▲	start
○	ch
•	slst
×	sc/UKdc
⊤	dc/UKtr
⋁	2 dc (UK2tr) in the same st
⊤	tr/UKdtr
△	end

Repeat from * to *.

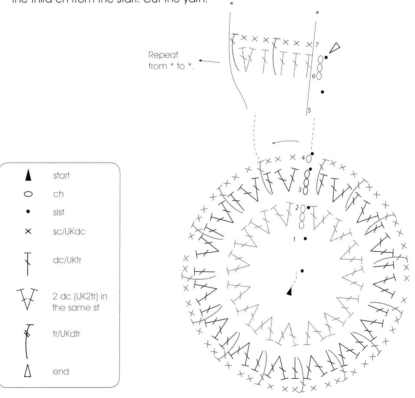

Shopping bag *

A practical and colourful big bag to hold your shopping.

MATERIALS

❋ Jersey yarn (bulky
   thickness): 1 ball of
   taupe and ½ ball
   each of fuchsia
   and pink
❋ N/15 (10mm)
   crochet hook

TECHNIQUE USED

Crochet

STITCHES USED

❋ Double crochet (dc)/
   UK treble (tr)
❋ Slip stitch (slst)
❋ Chain stitch (ch)
❋ Single crochet (sc)/
   UK double crochet
   (dc)

▲	start
○	ch
•	slst
⊤	dc/UKtr
⋎	2 dc (UK2tr) in the same st
△	end

With taupe yarn, make 18 ch, then work 5 ch to start the rectangle.

Round 1: 2 dc (UKtr) into the sixth ch from hook, 1 dc (UKtr) into each ch until the second-to-last ch of the foundation chain. Into the last ch: 2 dc (UKtr), 2 ch, 3 dc (UKtr), 2 ch, 2 dc (UKtr). On the other side of the foundation chain: 1 dc (UKtr) into each ch until the starting ch, which already contains 2 dc (UKtr) crocheted previously. Into this ch: 2 dc (UKtr), 2 ch, 2 dc (UKtr). End with 1 slst into the third ch of the 5 ch.

Round 2: 1 slst into the fourth ch of the 5 ch at the start of Round 1. 5 ch into the same place to start Round 2. 2 dc (UKtr) into the fifth ch of the 5 ch at the start of Round 1, 1 dc (UKtr) into each of the next stitches, continue until corner space formed in the previous round by 2 ch. Into this space: *2 dc (UKtr), 2 ch, 2 dc (UKtr),* 1 dc (UKtr) into each of the next dc (UKtr) of the previous round: you arrive at the second corner and you have done a long side and a short side of the rectangle. Rep from * to * hooking into the corner space, then 1 dc (UKtr) into each dc (UKtr) of the previous round until the next corner: you are on the third corner. Rep from * to *.
Continue with 1 dc (UKtr) into each dc (UKtr) of the previous round, then 2 dc (UKtr) into the slst at the end of round 1.
End with 1 slst into the fourth ch of the 5 ch at the start of Round 2.

Round 3: 5 ch into the same place to start Round 3. 2 dc (UKtr) into the fifth ch of the 5 ch at the start of Round 2, 1 dc (UKtr) into each of the next stitches, until the corner space formed in the previous round by 2 ch. Into this corner space: *2 dc (UKtr), 2 ch, 2 dc (UKtr)*, 1 dc (UKtr) into each of the next dc (UKtr) of the previous round: you arrive at the second corner and you have done a long side and a short side of the rectangle. Rep from * to * hooking into the corner space, then 1 dc (UKtr) into each dc (UKtr) of the previous round until the next corner: you are on the third corner. Rep from * to *. Continue with 1 dc (UKtr) into each dc (UKtr) of the previous round, then 2 dc (UKtr) into the slst at the end of Round 2.
End with 1 slst into the fourth ch of the 5 ch at the start of Round 3. You have 76 sts.

Rounds 4 and 5: 3 ch, 75 dc (UKtr). End with 1 slst into the third ch of the 5 ch at the start of round.
Cut the yarn.

Rounds 6 to 12: with fuchsia yarn: 3 ch, 75 dc (UKtr). End with 1 slst into the third ch of the 5 ch at the start of the round.
Cut the yarn.

Rounds 13 to 16: with pink yarn: 3 ch, 75 dc (UKtr). End with 1 slst into the third ch of the 5 ch at the start of round.
Cut the yarn.

Round 17: with taupe yarn: 1 ch, 75 sc (UKdc). End with 1 slst into the ch at the start of the round.

Round 18: 1 ch, 19 sc (UKdc). Continue with 27 ch (for the handles), 19 sc (UKdc), 27 ch. End with 1 slst in the ch at the start of the round.

Round 19: 1 ch, 90 sc (UKdc). End with 1 slst in the ch at the start of the round. Cut the yarn and fasten off.

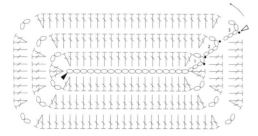

Cosy cat house **

With this cosy little house, your cat (or dog) can become the real star of the family.

MATERIALS

✳ *Jersey yarn (bulky thickness): ½ a ball each of royal blue, fuchsia and taupe*

✳ *Jersey yarn (medium thickness): remnants of orange*

✳ *N/15 (10mm) crochet hook*

✳ *Inner cardboard frame, length: 31cm (12in), height: 33cm (13in), depth: 34cm (13½in)*

✳ *Patterned material for the curtains: 40 x 80cm (15¾ x 31½in)*

✳ *Sewing needle*

TECHNIQUE USED
Crochet

STITCHES USED

✳ *Double crochet (dc)/ UK treble (tr)*

✳ *Chain stitch (ch)*

✳ *Single crochet (sc)/ UK double crochet (dc)*

The house consists of several panels that cover an inner cardboard frame. The panels are made from rows of double (UK treble) stitches.

THE TOP
Rows 1 to 10: with fuchsia yarn: 3 ch, 19 dc (UKtr).

THE BOTTOM
Rows 1 to 10: with royal blue yarn: 3 ch, 19 dc (UKtr).

THE SIDES AND THE BACK
Rows 1 to 5: with royal blue yarn: 3 ch, 19 dc (UKtr).
Rows 6 to 11: with taupe yarn: 3 ch, 19 dc (UKtr).

THE FRONT BANDS
The bottom band
Rows 1 and 2: with royal blue yarn: 3 ch, 19 dc (UKtr).
The top band
Rows 1 and 2: with taupe yarn: 3 ch, 19 dc (UKtr).

MAKING UP
1. Flatten out the squares and iron them into shape using a cloth.
2. With the orange yarn, assemble the multi-coloured panels of the sides and back, wrong side in, using 1 row of sc (UKdc). Put the blue section of the panels at the bottom.
3. Repeat the process for the top, bottom and front strips of the house. Put the blue strip at the bottom.
4. Cut the yarn and fasten off. Fit the crocheted cover around the supporting cardboard frame.

THE CURTAINS
1. Cut the fabric in half to get two 40cm (15¾in) squares, and sew a 2cm (¾in) hem all round.
2. Pleat your curtains using an iron, then sew them into position on the inside of the taupe-coloured band, using firm slip stitches.

Tip
The yarn from each colour change can be worked into the first stitches of the next row to give a perfect finish.

Draught excluder *

A draught excluder to keep your home warm in a deliciously vintage style.

44

MATERIALS
❋ Jersey yarn (bulky
   thickness): ½ a ball
   each of dark grey
   and yellow
❋ Jersey yarn (average
   thickness): ¼ a ball of
   China blue and
   remnants of black yarn
❋ N/15 (10mm)
   crochet hook
❋ size 15 (10mm)
   knitting needles
❋ Thread
❋ Sewing needle
❋ Stuffing

TECHNIQUES USED
Crochet and knitting

STITCHES USED
❋ Double crochet (dc)/
   UK treble (tr)
❋ Stocking stitch
❋ Slip stitch (slst)
❋ Chain stitch (ch)
❋ Single crochet (sc)/
   UK double crochet
   (dc)

The draught excluder is made up of two knitted rectangles assembled using double (UK treble) crochet stitches, to which two crocheted squares are added at the sides.

THE DRAUGHT EXCLUDER
1. With grey yarn, cast on 8 sts + 2 sts for the selvedge. Knit two rectangles the length of your draught excluder in stocking stitch: 1 row knitted on the right side, 1 row purled on the wrong side.
2. Flatten out the rectangles and iron them with a hot iron using a cloth. With yellow yarn: work 3 rows of double (UK treble) stitch along the long side of one of the rectangles. Repeat the process along the other long side.
3. Sew the top of the double (UK treble) stitching with firm stitches behind the edges of the long sides of the other grey rectangle, right sides together. The stitching will be inside the draught excluder.

SIDES OF DRAUGHT EXCLUDER
Make two squares following the diagram below. Always use a stitch marker to identify the last stitch of the round.

With China blue yarn: work 4 ch to form the starting ring, join with 1 slst.
Round 1: 1 ch, 8 sc (UKdc) into the starting ring.
Round 2: *1 sc (UKdc) into the next sc (UKdc), 3 sc (UKdc) into the next sc (UKdc).* Rep 3 times from * to *.
Round 3: *1 sc (UKdc) into each of the next 2 sc (UKdc), 3 sc (UKdc) into the next st, 1 sc (UKdc) into the next st.* Rep 3 times from * to *.
Round 4: *1 sc (UKdc) into each of the next 3 sc (UKdc), 3 sc (UKdc) into the next sc (UKdc), 1 sc (UKdc) into each of the next 2 sc (UKdc).* Rep 3 times from * to *.
Cut the yarn and fasten off.

MAKING UP
1. With black yarn, attach the square to the end of the draught excluder, wrong sides together, with 1 round of sc (UKdc). Crochet 3 sc (UKdc) in each of the corner stitches to give it a nice finish. Finish the work with 1 slst, cut the yarn and fasten off.
2. Stuff the draught excluder, then repeat Step 1 to attach the second side.

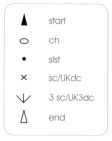

▲	start
○	ch
•	slst
×	sc/UKdc
↓	3 sc/UK3dc
Δ	end

Exotic jewellery *

Using a harmonious mixture of materials, this India-inspired design will ensure you stand out from the crowd.

MATERIALS

For the necklace

❊ Jersey yarn (medium thickness): Remnants of taupe

❊ N/15 (10mm) crochet hook

❊ Thread

❊ Sewing needle

❊ Large silver milgrain bead

❊ Small crackle porcelain bead

❊ Silver jewellery thread

❊ 2 small silver bead caps

❊ 2 large silver bead caps

❊ Jewellery pins

❊ Silver clasp

❊ Hook

❊ Wire cutters

❊ Jewellery pliers

❊ Flat-nosed pliers

TECHNIQUE USED

Crochet

STITCHES USED

❊ Double crochet (dc)/ UK treble (tr)

❊ Chain stitch (ch)

❊ Single crochet (sc)/ UK dc

❊ Solomon's Knot (sk)

THE NECKLACE

1. Cut eight x 50cm (19½in) lengths of the taupe coloured yarn. These strands will then be assembled using sc (UKdc) and sk.

2. With taupe yarn: 3 ch, 3 sc (UKdc) which wrap round the 8 strands then, *7cm (2¾in) further along the 8 strands, 1 sk, 2 sc (UKdc).* Rep 3 times from * to .* Then 1 sc (UKdc), 3 ch.

3. Cut the yarn that you are working with so that the whole piece is 50cm (19½in) long.

4. Distribute the sc (UKdc) and the sk regularly and symmetrically. The bead should be fixed on the first sc (UKdc) after the second sk.

5. Attaching the bead: slide a small bead cap onto the jewellery pin, followed by the porcelain bead, the milgrain bead and then a small bead cap to conceal the milgrain bead hole.

6. With wire cutters, cut the pin around 1cm (½in) from the cap. Hold the assembly firmly between thumb and forefinger, with your thumb under the beads. With jewellery pliers, bend the pin round to form the ring to attach it by (1).

7. Over-sew using small, firm stitches to attach the bead to the sc (UKdc) after the second sk.

8. Attaching the clasp: gather together the ends of the strands and use jewellery pliers to wrap them solidly together with the silver jewellery wire. Pass a jewellery pin inside the strands – it must protrude from the strands at each end. Squeeze the crimp very tight using flat-nosed pliers.

9. Thread a large bead cap onto the end of the pin protruding from the strands on each side. Cut the pin 1cm (½in) from the cap, then bend the pin round to form the ring to attach it by (2). Attach the clasp.

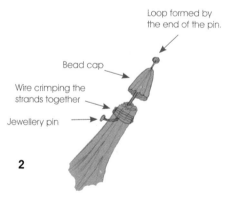

Loop formed by the end of the pin.

Bead cap

Wire crimping the strands together

Jewellery pin

2

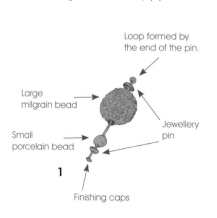

Loop formed by the end of the pin.

Large milgrain bead

Jewellery pin

Small porcelain bead

1

Finishing caps

MATERIALS

For the brooch

❊ Jersey yarn (medium
   thickness): remnants
   of fuchsia

❊ N/15 (10mm)
   crochet hook

❊ Large crackle
   porcelain bead

❊ Small faceted
   crystal bead

❊ 2 small silver
   bead caps

❊ Jewellery pin

❊ Silver hammered
   metal sequin

❊ Silver clasp

❊ Silver brooch pin

❊ Wire cutters

❊ Jewellery pliers

❊ Flat-nosed pliers

For the bracelet

❊ Jersey yarn (medium
   thickness): remnants
   of fuchsia, taupe
   or turquoise

❊ N/15 (10mm)
   crochet hook

❊ Large crackle porcelain,
   silver milgrain or
   celadon bead

TECHNIQUE USED

Crochet

STITCHES USED

❊ Double crochet (dc)/
   UK treble (tr)

❊ Slip stitch (slst)

❊ Chain stitch (ch)

❊ Single crochet (sc)/ UK dc

THE BROOCH

1. With fuchsia yarn, make 4 ch, join with 1 slst to form the small starting ring.

2. Crochet 14 dc (UKtr) sewn into the starting ring. Finish with 1 slst, cut the yarn and fasten off.

3. Using small stitches, over-sew the silver sequin into the centre of the round of double (UK treble) stitches.

4. Attaching the bead: slide a small bead cap onto the jewellery pin, followed by the small faceted crystal bead, the large porcelain bead and then another small bead cap to conceal the crackle porcelain bead hole.

5. With wire cutters, cut the pin 1cm (½in) from the cap. Hold the assembly firmly between thumb and forefinger, with your thumb under the beads. With jewellery pliers, bend the pin round to form the ring to attach it by (see diagram 1, page 46).

6. Using small stitches, firmly over-sew the bead onto the brooch.

7. Sew the brooch pin onto the back of the brooch, on the opposite side to the bead and perpendicular to the way it will hang so the brooch sits horizontally on your outfit.

THE BRACELET

1. Thread the bead onto the yarn.

2. Work 8 ch, fix the bead onto the bracelet using 1 sc (UKdc), then 8 ch.

3. Cut the yarn and join the two ends of the bracelet with an attractive double knot.

49

Laundry basket *

A solid and stylish basket to store your laundry.

MATERIALS

✳ *Jersey yarn (bulky thickness): 1 ball of light grey, 2 red balls and some remnants of fuchsia*

✳ *N/15 (10mm) crochet hook*

✳ *thread*

✳ *needle*

TECHNIQUE USED

Crochet

STITCHES USED

✳ *Double crochet (dc)/ UK treble (tr)*

✳ *Half-double (hdc)/ UK half-treble (htr)*

✳ *Slip stitch (slst)*

✳ *Chain stitch (ch)*

50

THE BASKET

With red yarn: make 5 ch, join with a slst to form the starting ring.

Round 1: 3 ch, 15 dc (UKtr) into the starting ring. End with 1 slst into the third ch from the start of the round.

Round 2: 3 ch, 1 dc (UKtr) between the slst ending Round 1 and the first dc (UKtr). 2 dc (UKtr) into each dc (UKtr) of the previous round. End with 1 slst into the third ch from the start of the round. You have 31 dc (UKtr).

Round 3: 3 ch, then for the next 2 sts: *2 dc (UKtr) into the first st, 1 dc (UKtr) into the next.* Rep 15 times from * to. * Make 2 dc (UKtr) into the last st, end with 1 slst

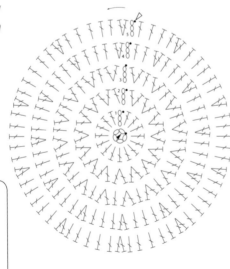

into the third ch at the start of the round. You have 47 dc (UKtr).

Round 4: 3 ch, then for the next 4 sts: *2 dc (UKtr) into the first st, 1 dc (UKtr) into each of the next 3 sts.*. Rep 10 times from * to *. You are left with 3 sts: 2 dc (UKtr) on the first st, 1 dc (UKtr) on the last 2 sts. End with 1 slst into the third ch from the start of the round. You have 59 dc (UKtr).

Round 5: 3 ch, then for the next 6 sts: *2 dc (UKtr) into the first st, 1 dc (UKtr) into each of the next 5 sts.*. Rep 8 times from * to *. You are left with 5 sts: *2 dc (UKtr) into the first st, then 1 dc (UKtr) into each of the remaining 4 sts.* End with 1 slst into the third ch from the start of the round. You have 69 dc (UKtr). You have finished the flat base. Start to make the basket's vertical walls.

Rows 6 to 9: 2 ch, 68 hdc (UKhtr). End with 1 slst into the second ch from the start of the round. Cut the yarn, leaving 10cm (4in). You have finished the red part of the basket.

Rows 10 to 27: with grey yarn: 2 ch, 68 hdc (UKhtr). End with 1 slst into the second ch from the start of the round.

THE HANDLE

With fuchsia yarn, make 15 ch, join with a slst to form the starting ring.

Round 1: 3 ch, 45 dc (UKtr) into the starting ring. End with 1 slst into the third ch from the start of the round. Cut the yarn and fasten off. Attach the handle to the body of the basket using slip stitch, positioned so half the handle is visible above the basket.

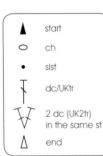

▲	start
o	ch
•	slst
⊤	dc/UKtr
V	2 dc (UK2tr) in the same st
∆	end

Geometric floor mat   *

These round motifs fit together to make any shape you wish.

MATERIALS

* Jersey yarn (medium
  thickness): 1 ball
  each of electric
  blue, navy blue, royal
  blue, light grey, dark
  grey, pink, red
  and taupe
* N/15 (10mm)
  crochet hook

TECHNIQUE USED

Crochet

STITCHES USED

* Double crochet (dc)/
  UK treble (tr)
* Slip stitch (slst)
* Chain stitch (ch)

The mat consists of 31 circles and measures around 120 x 90cm (47 x 35½in). Feel free to adapt the number of circles to the size of mat that you want.

FOR EACH CIRCLE

Make 5 ch, join with 1 slst to form the starting ring.

Round 1: 3 ch, 15 dc (UKtr) into the starting ring. End with 1 slst into the third ch from the start of the round.

Round 2 (for half the mat's circles): 3 ch, 1 dc (UKtr) between the slst ending round 1 and the first dc (UKtr). 2 dc (UKtr) into each dc (UKtr) of the previous round. End with 1 slst into the third ch from the start of the round. You have 31 dc (UKtr). Fasten off.

Flatten out the rounds and iron them into shape with a hot iron using a cloth. Allow to dry.

MAKING UP

1. Assemble the circles by knotting them together with a piece of grey yarn at the back of the work.

2. Work in the ends of the yarn.

> **Tip**
> Put the pieces of your mat together on the floor before starting to join up the circles so you can check that the spaces between the rounds are even.

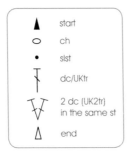

▲	start
○	ch
•	slst
⊤	dc/UKtr
⋎	2 dc (UK2tr) in the same st
△	end

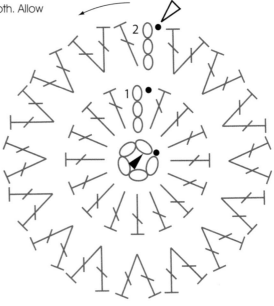

Two-colour basket *

A round, multi-purpose basket, made in whatever colours you like.

MATERIALS

* *Jersey yarn (bulky thickness): 1 ball of royal blue*
* *Jersey yarn (medium thickness): 1 ball of fuchsia*
* *10mm (N/15) crochet hook*

TECHNIQUE USED

Crochet

STITCHES USED

* *Treble (tr)/ US Double crochet (dc)*
* *Slip stitch (slst)*
* *Chain stitch (ch)*
* *Double crochet (dc)/ US Single crochet (sc)*

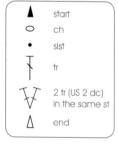

▲	start
o	ch
•	slst
⊤	tr
V	2 tr (US 2 dc) in the same st
Δ	end

With fuchsia yarn, make 5 ch, join with a slst to form the starting ring.

Round 1: 3 ch, 15 dc (UKtr) into the starting ring. End with 1 slst into the third ch from the start of the row.

Round 2: 3 ch, 1 dc (UKtr) between the slst joining round 1 and the first dc (UKtr). 2 dc (UKtr) into each dc (UKtr) of the previous round. End with 1 slst into the third ch from the start of the round. You have 31 dc (UKtr).

Round 3: 3 ch, then into the next 2 sts: *2 dc (UKtr) into the first st, 1 dc (UKtr) into the next.* Rep 15 times from * to.* Make 2 dc (UKtr) into the last st, end with 1 slst into the third ch from the start of the round. You have 47 dc (UKtr).

Round 4: 3 ch, then into the next 4 sts: *2 dc (UKtr) into the first st, 1 dc (UKtr) into each of the next 3 sts.* Rep 10 times from * to.* You have 3 sts left: 2 dc (UKtr) on the first st, 1 dc (UKtr) on the last 2 sts. End with 1 slst into the third ch from the start of the round. You have 59 dc (UKtr).

Round 5: 3 ch, then into the next 6 sts: *2 dc (UKtr) into the first st, 1 dc (UKtr) into each of the next 5 sts.* Rep

8 times from * to.* You are left with 5 sts: 2 dc (UKtr) into the first st, then 1 dc (UKtr) into each of the remaining 4 sts. End with 1 slst into the third ch from the start of the round. You have 69 dc (UKtr).

Cut the yarn, leaving around 10cm (4in). Flatten out and press into shape with a hot iron using a press cloth. Allow to dry.

Round 6: with blue yarn: 1 ch, then 68 sc (UKdc). Make sure you work the fuchsia yarn into the first blue sc (UKdc)s to hide it. End with 1 slst.

Round 7: 1 ch, 68 sc (UKdc). End with 1 slst.

Round 8: 1 ch, 68 sc (UKdc). End with 1 slst.

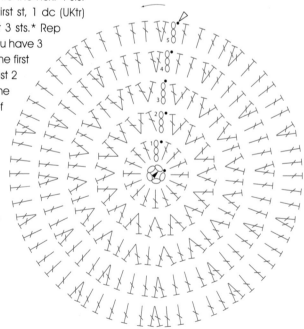

Beaded door curtain *

A decorative addition to any doorway in your home!

56

MATERIALS

* Jersey yarn (medium thickness): 1 ball of royal blue
* N/15 (10mm) crochet hook
* Embroidery needle
* 5 large, multi-coloured wooden beads per strand

TECHNIQUE USED
Crochet

STITCHES USED

* Chain stitch (ch)
* Single crochet (sc)/ UK double crochet (dc)
* Solomon's Knot (sk)

ONE STRAND

1. With an embroidery needle, thread 5 beads onto the yarn.
2. Start to crochet the strand: 2 ch, *3 or 4 sk spaced around 5-8cm (2-3in) apart, then attach a bead using 1 sc (UKdc).* Rep * to * 5-6 times.
3. Finish with a few sk depending on how long the strands need to be for the height of the door. Cut the yarn.

Once assembled, the strands are spaced around 8cm (3in) apart. You therefore need 10 strands for a door that is 80cm (31½in) wide. Calculate how many strands you need for the width of the door.

MAKING UP

1. Work a foundation chain the width of your door and then work one row of double (UK treble) stitches.
2. Sew the strands solidly onto the row of double (UK treble) stitches, and then fix it on top of the door aperture.

Tip
Vary the bead colour and spacing to achieve the look you want for your door curtain.

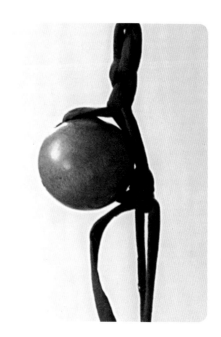

Sofa pillow ***

An explosion of colour and texture – you are bound to love this vibrant pillow.

MATERIALS

❋ Jersey yarn (medium or bulky thickness): ¼ ball each of navy blue, royal blue, fuchsia, light grey, dark grey, orange, pink, red and taupe

❋ N/15 (10mm) crochet hook

❋ size 15 (10mm) knitting needles

❋ 75cm (29½in) square cushion slip

TECHNIQUE USED

Crochet and knitting

STITCHES USED

❋ Double crochet (dc)/ UK treble (tr)

❋ Half-double (hdc)/ UK half-treble (htr)

❋ Treble (tr)/ UK double treble (dtr)

❋ Chain stitch (ch)

❋ Single crochet (sc)/ UK double crochet (dc)

❋ Garter stitch

THE ORANGE & TAUPE BAND (KNITTED)

Cast 16 stitches onto your needle: 14 sts + 1 st on each side for the selvedge. Using garter stitch (see page 13), 1 row pearl, knit *3 rows taupe, 3 rows orange.* Repeat another 6 times from * to. * You get a striped taupe and orange band, with a selvedge of 42 sts. Give it a quick iron using a cloth to flatten and shape the band.

THE CROCHET PATTERN

Crochet the pattern onto one of the long sides of the band (see diagram page 61). Worked using 6 sts, the pattern is repeated 6 times to get a 42 st rectangle over 16 rows. Start the pattern by hooking into the stitches of the knitted strip's selvedge.

Row 1: with light grey yarn: 1 ch, 41 sc (UKdc). Fasten off and cut the yarn.

Row 2: 3 ch, 41 dc (UKtr). Fasten off and cut the yarn.

Row 3: with navy blue yarn: 1 ch, 2 sc (UKdc), 3 dc (UKtr), hooking into the sc (UKdc) of Row 1, *3 sc (UKdc), 3 dc (UKtr) hooking into the sc (UKdc) of Row 1.* Rep 6 times from * to.* Fasten off and cut the yarn.

Row 4: with dark grey yarn: 1 ch, 41 sc (UKdc). Fasten off and cut the yarn.

Row 5: 3 ch, 41 dc (UKtr). Fasten off and cut the yarn.

Row 6: with navy blue yarn: *3 dc (UKtr) hooking into the sc (UKdc) of Row 4, 3 sc (UKdc)*. Rep 6 times from * to. * Fasten off and cut the yarn.

Row 7: with pink yarn: 1 ch, 41 sc (UKdc).

Fasten off and cut the yarn.

Row 8: 1 ch, 1 hdc (UKhtr), 1 dc (UKtr), 1 tr (UKdtr), 1 dc (UKtr), 1 hdc (UKhtr), *1 sc (UKdc), 1 hdc (UKhtr), 1 dc (UKtr), 1 tr (UKdtr), 1 dc (UKtr), 1 hdc (UKhtr).* Rep 6 times from * to. * Fasten off and cut the yarn.

Row 9: with royal blue yarn: 4 ch, 1 dc (UKtr), 1 hdc (UKhtr), 1 sc (UKdc), 1 hdc (UKhtr), 1 dc (UKtr), *1 tr (UKdtr), 1 dc (UKtr), 1 hdc (UKhtr), 1 sc (UKdc), 1 hdc (UKhtr), 1 dc (UKtr).* Rep 6 times from * to. * Fasten off and cut the yarn.

Row 10: 1 ch, 41 sc (UKdc). Fasten off and cut the yarn.

Row 11: with taupe yarn: 3 ch, 41 dc (UKtr). Fasten off and cut the yarn.

Row 12: 3 ch, 41 dc (UKtr). Fasten off and cut the yarn.

Row 13: with orange yarn: 1 ch, 41 sc (UKdc). Fasten off and cut the yarn.

Row 14: with fuchsia yarn: 3 ch, 41 dc (UKtr). Fasten off and cut the yarn.

Row 15: with orange yarn: 1 ch, 41 sc (UKdc). Fasten off and cut the yarn.

Row 16: with fuchsia yarn: 3 ch, 41 dc (UKtr). Fasten off and cut the yarn. Crochet the other part of the pattern by hooking into the stitches on the other long side of the knitted band.

Rows 1 to 5: with royal blue yarn: 1 ch, 41 sc (UKdc). Fasten off and cut the yarn.

Row 6: with fuchsia yarn: 1 ch, 41 sc (UKdc). Fasten off and cut the yarn.

Row 7: with grey yarn: 3 ch, 41 dc (UKtr). Fasten off and cut the yarn.

Row 8: with fuchsia yarn: 1 ch, 41 sc (UKdc). Fasten off and cut the yarn.

You will have a square measuring 75cm (29½in) along each side.

Flatten out the square and iron it into shape using a cloth.

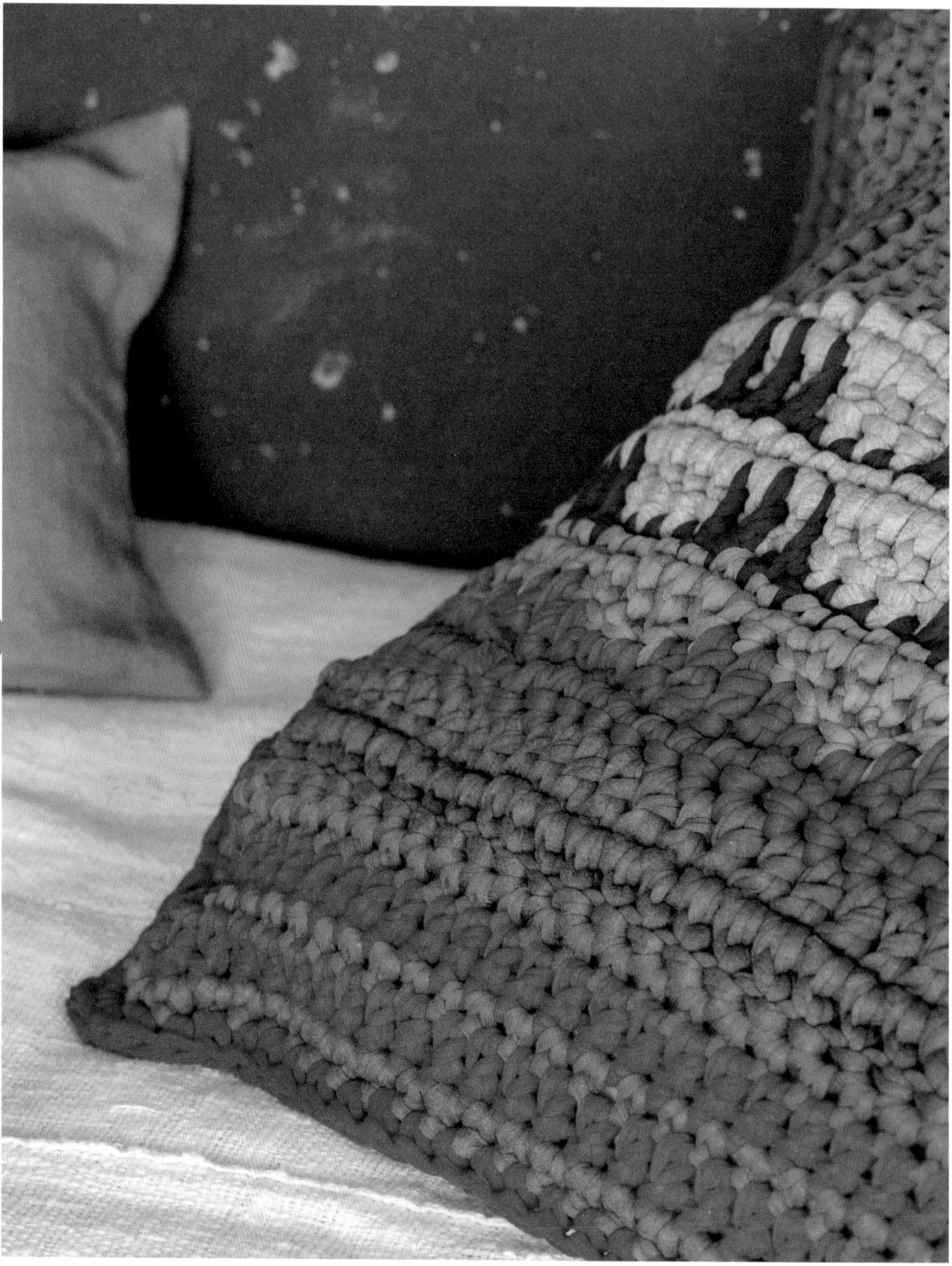

THE BORDER

1. Crochet 1 row of sc (UKdc) in taupe, then 1 row of sc (UKdc) in red. Work all the cut ends of yarn into the sc (UKdc) in order to get a neat finish.

2. Make sure you form neat corners by always using 3 sc (UKdc) at each corner stitch.

3. Give it another iron with a cloth to flatten it out again. Cut the yarn and fasten off.

MAKING UP

Sew the square you have made onto a cushion slip using invisible stitching.
You could also make the cushion slip yourself, adapting it to the size of your work.

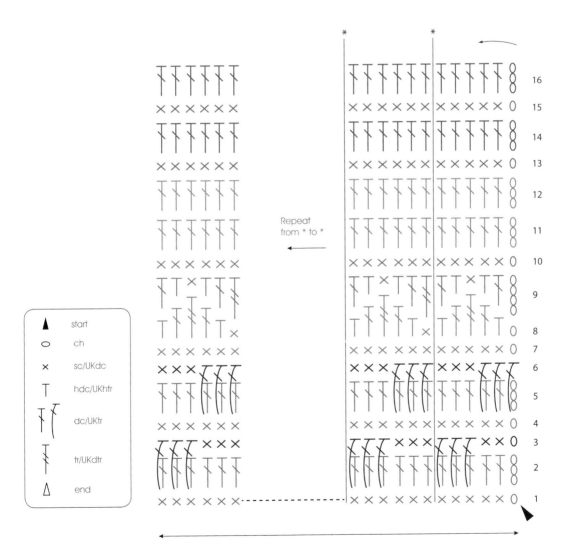

Repeat from * to *

▲	start
○	ch
×	sc/UKdc
T	hdc/UKhtr
⊤⊤	dc/UKtr
⊤	tr/UKdtr
Δ	end

42 sts

Lily Handbag **

A beautiful bag to carry all your secrets.

MATERIALS

❋ Jersey yarn (average or bulky thickness):
½ a ball each of fuchsia, light grey, black and mottled pink

❋ N/15 (10mm) crochet hook

TECHNIQUE USED

Crochet

STITCHES USED

❋ Double crochet (dc)/ UK treble (tr)

❋ Slip stitch (slst)

❋ Chain stitch (ch)

❋ Single crochet (sc)/ UK double crochet (dc)

62

THE BODY OF THE BAG

Worked in rows. Each time you change yarn colour, cut the previous yarn, leaving a strand of around 10cm (4in).

With pink yarn, make 24 ch.

Row 1: 3 ch, 24 dc (UKtr). Turn the work round.

Row 2: 3 ch, 24 dc (UKtr). Turn the work round.

Row 3: with black yarn: 1 ch, 24 sc (UKdc). Turn the work round.

Row 4: with fuchsia yarn: *1 ch, 3 sc (UKdc), 1 dc (UKtr) in the same place, hooking into the dc (UKtr) of Row 2.* Rep 7 times from * to. * Turn the work round. You have worked 24 sc (UKdc) + 8 dc (UKtr): you have therefore worked 32 sts. In the next row , you need to stop at 24 sts.

Row 5: with grey yarn: 3 ch, *3dc (UKtr), skip 1 st.*. Rep 7 times from * to. * You have 24 sts. Turn the work round.

Row 6: 3 ch, 24 dc (UKtr). Turn the work round.

Row 7: with fuchsia yarn: 1 ch, 24 sc (UKdc). Turn the work round.

Row 8: with black yarn: *1 ch, 3 sc (UKdc), 1 dc (UKtr) in the same place, hooking into the dc (UKtr) of Row 6*. Rep 7 times from * to. * You have done 24 sc (UKdc) + 8 dc (UKtr): you have therefore worked 32 sts. In the next row, you need to stop at 24 sts.

The basic pattern is done. Rep Rows 1-8 three times: you have 24 rows.

Repeat Rows 1 and 2 again so you have the same colour on each side of the opening when you fold the rectangle in two to form the body of the bag. You have 26 rows.

With the grey yarn, make a border of two rows of sc (UKdc) round the panel you have just crocheted, working the colour change strands into Row 1 so they are hidden. Make sure you work 3 sc (UKdc) into each corner to ensure you have proper right angles. The shorter side of the panel is 28 sc (UKdc) long, including the border.

Flatten out the rectangle and iron it into shape using a cloth.

Repeat from * to * ⟶

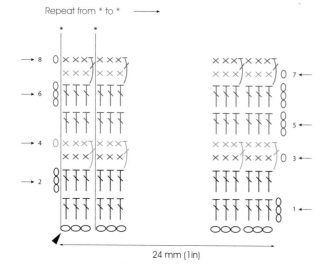

24 mm (1in)

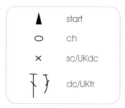

▲	start
○	ch
×	sc/UKdc
⊤	dc/UKtr

THE SIDES OF THE BAG

Make two triangles, one for each side of the bag.

With fuchsia yarn, make 4 ch, join with 1 slst to form the starting ring.

Round 1: 3 ch, 2 dc (UKtr) hooking into the ring, 4 ch, 3 dc (UKtr) hooking into the ring, 4 ch, 3 dc (UKtr) hooking into the ring, 4 ch. End with 1 slst.

Round 2: 3 ch, 2 dc (UKtr), *3 dc (UKtr) hooking into the space in the 4 ch of the previous round, 4 ch, 3 dc (UKtr) hooking into the spaces in the 4 ch of the previous round,* 3 dc (UKtr). Rep from * to.* 3 dc (UKtr), rep from * a.* Finish with 1 slst, cut the yarn.

> **Tip**
> *Instead of making a knot with the jersey yarn, you could sew on a bow made from ribbon.*

▲	start
○	ch
•	slst
⊤	dc/UKtr
V	2 dc (UK2tr) in the same st
△	end

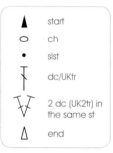
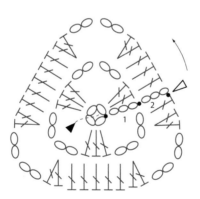

MAKING UP

1. Fold the rectangle into half to find the middle of the long sides. Mark the middle with pins.

2. Find the middle of one side of one of the triangles and mark it with a pin. Pin the triangles into place on the rectangle, wrong sides together, lining up the marked middles. Make sure it all looks nice and symmetrical.

3. Crochet together using black yarn: bend the rectangle into half, back to back. From the top corner of the rectangle, assemble the sides by working 10 sc (UKdc) hooking into the outside strand of the grey sc (UKdc) of the rectangle's border. You reach the point of the triangle.

4. Attach the triangle to the rectangle by working sc (UKdc) all round the triangle, hooking into the outside strands of the border of the panel and the outside round of the triangle. Finish with 1 slst, cut the yarn and fasten off.

THE TOP OF THE BAG

Start at the top right-hand corner.

Round 1: With black yarn: 56 sc (UKdc), end with 1 slst.

Round 2: 4 sc (UKdc), 28 ch, 8 sc (UKdc), 28 ch, 4 sc (UKdc). You have formed the bag's handles.

Round 3: 72 sc (UKdc) around the rim of the bag, up round the handles and then continue along the rim, end with 1 slst. Cut the yarn and fasten off.

Make a pretty double bow into the top right-hand corner of the bag.